Never Again—But Wait… Did You Consult God?

Author Kenya Herring-Walker

NEVER AGAIN

But Wait... Did You Consult God?

Author Kenya Herring-Walker

Pearly Gates Publishing, LLC, Houston, Texas (USA)

Never Again—But Wait… Did You Consult God?

Never Again:
But Wait… Did You Consult God?

Copyright © 2021
Kenya Herring-Walker

All Rights Reserved.
No portion of this publication may be reproduced, stored in an electronic system, or transmitted in any form or by any means (electronic, mechanical, photocopy, recording, or otherwise) without written permission from the author or publisher. Brief quotations may be used in literary reviews.

Print ISBN 13: 978-1-948853-16-3
Digital ISBN 13: 978-1-948853-17-0
Library of Congress Control Number: 2020922022

Scripture references are taken from the English Standard Version (ESV) of the Holy Bible and used with permission via Zondervan at Biblegateway.com. Public Domain.

For information and bulk ordering, contact:
Pearly Gates Publishing, LLC
Angela Edwards, CEO
P.O. Box 62287
Houston, TX 77205
BestSeller@PearlyGatesPublishing.com

Author Kenya Herring-Walker

In Loving Memory...

Maxine McQuay

Never Again—But Wait… Did You Consult God?

Mr. and Mrs. Issac Walker

Author Kenya Herring-Walker

Dedication

This book is dedicated to my late and beloved mother,
Maxine McQuay.

Mama, I truly miss you. I remember the moment while we waited for your medicine to be filled and I took that time to share with you the manuscript of my book. I began to read it aloud to you (as I chucked and smiled) and, by the time I finished reading the first chapters, you looked at me with such a serious and inquiring stare and asked, "Kenya, you're going to tell them people all your business?!" I reassured you that as our Lord and Savior instructed me to give it, I would deliver every ounce — leaving not one rock unturned.

Mama, thank you for being my rock of reason in everything you have shown me — support, love, and the strength to keep going. Until we meet again, I will hold you in my heart on earth.

Love Your Baby,
Sugarmama/Granny

Acknowledgments

First, giving all honor, glory, and praise to my **Lord and Savior Jesus Christ** who is the Headship over my life. Without You in my life, I truly do not know where I would be. Lord, I just thank You for shielding and protecting my family and me from all hurt, harm, and danger. Thank You for keeping me in my right mind so that I could live to tell my testimonies of how You have forever brought me over and out of my painful situations. Abba, thank You.

To my Fab5: I love each of you to no end. Besides giving my life to Christ, giving birth to each of you has been by far the best thing to ever happen in my life. You all are the reason I have always pushed, pulled, and persevered. You have molded and made me the mother I am today. Always remember that Mama will always do what she can — within her power — to shield and protect you from any danger. I love you all.

To my Siblings — Fredricka, Anita, and Willie: Thank you for always believing in and supporting me in all the things I set my mind and hands to do. Each of you holds a place in my heart where only blood siblings could ever reside (LOL!). Willie (Fatdaddy), I could write a book about you, brother. You have been my voice of reason since day one. You have been a father to me when daddy was not around. You have been a friend when I needed one. You have been such a great role model in my life, and I just want to take this moment to say thank you for it all. No matter how many differences you and I have had in the past (as most siblings do), you have always been there when I needed you the most. Brother, thank you. I love you.

To my beautiful, smart, and God-fearing Niece, Curtel: Thank you for always having my back when I needed you the most. It was an honor helping Mama raise you and your sister into the beautiful young ladies you are today. Curtel, you have always been the niece who wanted to always be on my hip and heels. You would not allow me out of your sight. Although you are my niece, it feels as though you are more like my little sister. I love you.

To one of my Best Friends, Robyn Moe: Friend, thank you for being a true friend from day one. No matter when, time and again you have shown me that right comes before wrong. You walked with me through the fires of life that were sent to consume and kill me. Friend, I owe you my very life, but being that I can't give it, I will keep living and loving you as my best friend. I love you. You helped save my life, and I will never forget it.

To my late Pastor and Beloved Wife, Elder Harold Franklin and Sister Michelle Franklin: Thank you for loving my family from day one as your very own and for embracing and nurturing us to spiritual health. We love you so much. I can hear you now, Pastor: *"Some things you need to take to your grave."* (LOL!) Pastor, you would have been very proud.

To my Father, Willie Herring, Sr.: Daddy, I love you so much. Thank you for always loving me past every disappointment. I know that life has its way of "happening," but I now know those disappointments have helped me to be whom God created me to be. Daddy, thank you for being such a good father to me. Now that Mama has gained her wings, you have some large shoes to fill! I love you, Daddy.

Saving the best for last… **To my Husband, Prayer Partner, Best Friend, and Spiritual War Partner, Issac:** Honey, thank you for not abandoning us. You are such an amazing husband and father. Baby, until my last breath, I will forever be grateful for you and honor you. Thank you for reviving that which I thought was impossible and a lost cause. Thank you for loving me beyond the hurt you had to endure while chasing after me. I promise that your heart is now safe and secure with me. You have my lifetime of undivided attention. Everything I tried to look for in a man, you already possess—and baby, I am enjoying it all! Ask me again, and I would stand on the mountaintops of Heaven and say, *"I LOVE YOU!"*

Encouraging Word

In the Word of God, it simply reminds us that everything has its time and season, but we know when that season is up, that "thing" must go. When looking back over your life, stop regretting the things that have taken place and start thanking God for growth. There has been so much that I regret, but in the same breath, so much that I have learned.

I must ask you this: How much have you matured since your last testimony?

It's time we move forward in the coming chapters. Be prepared to take notes along the way. Remember: Your journey is not about you. It's about the people who are standing in your spiritual line behind you, waiting for you to move forward and not be stagnated.

Move… Forward… You are holding up the line! All that you're enduring had to happen in order to push you into your **PURPOSE!**

Let Us Pray

Most Heavenly Father,

We come with stretched out hands and lifted voices to first say, *"Thank You, Father!"* We thank You for forgiving us of our repeated offenses. We thank You for being the Watcher and Deliverer of our souls. Father, we thank You for our Brother, Jesus Christ, who died and rose on the third day so that we would have a chance of everlasting life.

We ask You, Father, that this book and testimonies within will help the readers to draw nigh unto You and surrender their plans for Your plans. We ask that each reader not only be a reader, but also a doer of Your words that are written in this book as they live their lives on purpose, leaning and truly depending on You. As we prepare to read, we ask that You open their eyes so that they can see spiritually. Open their ears so that they can hear what You are saying, even unto them. Lastly, Father, open their mouths so that they will tell the world where and how far You have brought them from, being unashamed and aware.

Father, thank You. In all this we ask of You, knowing that our prayers have been answered.

In Jesus' Matchless Name, we do pray.

Amen.

Author Kenya Herring-Walker

Introduction

In our humanness, many of us often judge others and say what we would not tolerate or do based on what we see going on in their lives with our natural eyes. We must be ever so careful with the words we use. Proverbs says that death and life are in the power of the tongue and they that love it shall eat the fruits thereof. Use your words wisely and know that every word spoken is accounted for by God. *"I tell you, on the day of judgment, people will give account for every careless word they speak, for by your words you will be justified, and by your words, you will be condemned"* (Matthew 12:36-37, ESV).

In the Word of God (John 8:1-11), it gives an account of an adulteress woman. Teachers of the law and the Pharisees brought the adulteress woman to stand in shame before Jesus in hopes to stone her to death from being caught in the VERY act of adultery. Jesus simply told them, *"He without sin, cast the first stone."* The moral of that biblical account is this: We all have shortcomings, sin, and fall short of the glory of God.

So, hold your stone.

Never Again—But Wait… Did You Consult God?

Think for a moment and reflect on your life. Are there things you said you would **NEVER** do? Are there things you have settled for, yet you previously said, *"I would **NEVER**!"* Before you say what you would **NEVER** do, I encourage you to first ask the Lord, *"Father God, what is it YOU would have for me to do?"*

Remember this: There is a time and a season for everything. When that season is over, that "thing" must go! The pain you endure is not your own. It is for the next person standing in the spiritual line behind you. Even the pain that our Lord and Savior bore, He did so until death. He did it for a reason, and when His time came to be crucified, it was finished.

There have been times when I professed my love for the Lord but forgot to ask Him for permission to do certain things in my life. It's funny how we can go and ask people we trust what we think about "this" or "that," but we forget to ask God — the One who holds all power in His hands over our lives. There were many times in my life when I was in a place of uncertainty…places where a lot of my overdue seasons had taken place. I know I have missed out on so much, including the timely blessings the Lord had stored away just for me. I thank God for not forgetting about me, even amid all my woes, putting Him on the back burner, and just "doing me" (as the younger generation would say). I thank the Lord for delivering me from my woes and the rocks of my foes.

God has not forgotten about you, either. He is the same God yesterday, today, and forever and will deliver you right now—right where you sit or stand. Despite what it looks like, know there is still hope. God desires that you **LIVE** and are **HAPPY!**

We were not placed on this earth to be abused in any shape, form, or fashion. I can attest to that because I am a survivor…and you can be one, too! For many years, I thought the abuse I received was "true love." If they did not beat me, they did not love me. If that is you, please stop sitting in silence. Reach out for the help you need. You are worth far more than what you are settling for.

My prayer is that my testimony blesses and enlightens you on this journey called "life."

Never Again—But Wait… Did You Consult God?

Be **STRONG**. BE **BOLD**. Be **BRAVE**. God has already **WON** the battle! Be encouraged, knowing that He will also win the **WAR**. We all will **OVERCOME** our struggles. The best part about overcoming is that God is and always will be with us every step of the way, for He said He would never leave us nor forsake us. God said that He would be with us until the very end. Do not give up. We have all been faced with heartbreaking challenges and news. Maybe you faced a family feud, the death of a loved one, unemployment, or the effects of the COVID-19 pandemic. I need you to take note and remember this: No matter what you are faced with, you will come out on the other side as a bigger and better person. It is not over concerning you. Whether it takes you a month or a lifetime, your learning experience can be passed along to others. Let us face it: God will never allow too much to rest on our shoulders that He knows is too heavy for us to bear. I know that you may say, "If I had a chance to do things over, I would," but I need you to know that your situation has caused and will cause others to grow in similar situations. Your life is not about you. Rather, it is about those standing behind you who are waiting for their breakthrough.

> *"It's not about where you have been but where you are going.*
> *Never allow your past to suppress you.*
> *You're a diamond that is eager to shine!"*
> **~ Author Kenya Herring-Walker ~**

Author Kenya Herring-Walker

Table of Contents

In Loving Memory... vi

Dedication viii

Acknowledgments ix

Encouraging Word xii

Let Us Pray xiii

Introduction xiv

Chapter One 1

Chapter Two 12

Chapter Three 20

Chapter Four 28

Chapter Five 39

Chapter Six 47

Chapter Seven 55

Chapter Eight 62

Chapter Nine 72

Chapter Ten 81

Let's Wrap This One Up! 83

Closing Prayer 84

About the Author 85

Chapter One

When you put others before God and love them the most, they will make you wring your hands and cry. Never put anyone or anything before God. If you do, it will bring the bittersweetness of your life to the surface.

It was the month of July — the hottest time of the year. I was five months pregnant with my fifth child…and alone. I promised myself I would **NEVER** allow myself to be put in that position again. Single. Pregnant. Unwed. Geesh. Besides having baby after baby, wasn't I good enough to be someone's *wife?*

Being a single parent yet again made me become bitter and angry with myself. I had to constantly tell myself, *"Kenya, get it together. You are pretty, young, and have a bright future ahead of you. Why do you keep going through this same never-ending cycle?"* How in the world did I find myself in the grips of **ENTANGLEMENT** again? I trusted and loved Kendrick — the man who impregnated me. When I cried out to God, **"WHY???"** — I knew I had put myself in that situation but was in denial. I could not believe another man had wiggled out of the grips of my love while leaving behind a package that said, *"I was here."*

Another baby to care for without a father… *Sigh.*

My faith in God was at an all-time low at the time. Now that I think about it, I had no faith at all. None. Not even mustard-seed faith as Matthew 17:20 tells us to have. It was as if my life was in a storm in the middle of the Gulf of Mexico.

No paddle. No lights. Just total darkness all around, with no sign of rescue coming for me. Peter had a better chance of walking on water with Jesus without almost drowning before my faith would have surfaced anywhere. If only I had waited on the Lord, He would have heard my cry. But no, I had to do things my way yet again. I was in such a dark, cold, and lonely place. Nowhere in the recesses of my mind did I envision the life I was living. In that place, I did not even feel the land where I could at least try to find some help. Sadly, the water appeared endless as it stretched out before me. The sounds of the water as it clashed together, almost in hopes of swallowing me up, were resounding. There was no one around to witness the very pit I felt I was in. It was almost as if I were being forced to look at and reflect on my life without interruption. No phone. No family. No friends. And no lovers.

When I could muster up the strength to repeatedly say, *"Jesus...Jesus...Help me, Jesus!"* relief continued to elude me. It was just me inside of my spiritual boat with one paddle, no fresh water to drink, no food to eat, and no visual signs of help.

I recall the multiple attempts I made to self-abort my unborn child. I remember during naptime as a child, when my aunties' favorite daytime shows would come on, that would be when I had to take a nap so that they would not miss a beat of what was happening on the TV. I also remember hearing the latest gossip about other family members' personal business, including about how someone could not afford to have an abortion, so they decided to self-abort with the use of a hanger. *Fast-forward….* I found a metal hanger and shortened it. I got completely naked and straddled my toilet to try to do as I heard the "procedure" should happen. My legs began to shake as I eased the cold metal into my vagina. The deeper in it went, it caused me to urinate. I then gave up and cried. I yelled out, "**I CANNOT DO THIS!** *Why is it so hard to do something so simple? God, I need Your help!*" I then wiped myself, at which time I saw a spot of blood, so I jumped into the shower. (Remembering those gruesome thoughts makes my skin crawl and has me repeatedly asking God for forgiveness.) I did not want to be stuck with caring for a baby I did not make myself and did not want.

One month before I learned I was pregnant again, I had gone to the clinic and aborted my other child. As I laid there on that cold table, it appeared none of the medicine the doctor gave me worked to ease my pain. I laid there and vowed to the Lord, "*Father, if you see me through this abortion, I promise I won't have anymore."* The Lord spoke to me in the tone of a parent who was fed up with their child's lies and broken promises:

"Kenya, you shall feel every effect of this abortion, for you know it is wrong to kill. How long will you keep repeating the same thing over and over again? Haven't I heard all this before?"

The Word of God tells us it is better not to make a vow than to make one and break it.

As I laid there with my legs wide open, the doctor worked his way through the procedure with his utensils and vacuum. I felt every tug, vibration, pull, and pinch. I asked the doctor for more medicine, but there was only so much he could give me. Oh, gosh! It hurt so **BAD**! I began to moan and groan because I had never felt pain like that before. The tears streamed down the side of my face and were warmer than the utensils the doctor used. Once in the recovery room, I was offered graham crackers and juice—neither of which I wanted. All I wanted was for the pain to be gone.

When I was released, my plans were to leave Kendrick alone altogether, but when he called, I went to him. I really did not know how to tell him about the "little visit to the clinic." Did he really deserve to know? There were many red flags that flapped wildly concerning him, which is why I could not see having a baby by him. There was something very secretive about Kendrick that I could not put my finger on.

That very night after my abortion, we had sex yet again—unwed and unprotected. As Kendrick was having his way with me, I stared at the ceiling and began to repent to God for yet another broken promise. The Holy Spirit instantly brought back to my remembrance all that God had spoken to me. I knew there would be a hefty price to pay. I wanted to push Kendrick off me, ball up, and cry...but I didn't. As soon as he finished, I rolled over, took a fistful of the cover, and placed it in my mouth so that I could cry silently without him noticing. As I laid there, he pulled me close to him, positioning himself for the rest of the night's rest. Meanwhile, I did not want to be touched or held in any way, shape, or form. I just wanted to be left completely alone.

Just as expected, I learned I was pregnant again roughly a month after the abortion. I hung my head low and didn't dare utter a word of prayer because of the shame I felt. Besides, I kept making promises to God that I wouldn't do "this" or "that," and was a total failure. I felt unworthy of approaching the Father's throne for anything. It was like walking in mud and then coming into my mom's house with wall-to-wall white carpet. I felt "dirtied up" and knew I didn't belong somewhere so beautiful. So, just like everything else in my life, I dealt with it as best I could.

When I was five months pregnant with Maxine, Kendrick and I went on one of his softball trips. After that trip was when the relationship between he and I took a totally unexpected turn. Upon our return, I drove him home (an apartment he shared with his cousin), and I returned to the apartment I shared with my best friend Issac. My other children were there as well. After spending time with my children and settling down for the night, I called Kendrick repeatedly, but he would not answer. I even sent back-to-back texts, none of which he responded to. It was so unlike him. What was really going on?

I later learned that he had gathered his belongings and moved back down south to be a father to his last abandonment. (Sigh.)

I vowed to myself at that point, **"NEVER AGAIN,"** but did not consult God about a thing. Nonetheless, I said that was it. I was done. It was final. I refused to allow myself to be used and abused by another man. I would simply do as they do and say as they say, all while keeping it moving without any packages being left behind and no strings attached.

At least I *thought* it was final…

Chapter 1 Points to Ponder

1. Where did Kenya go wrong?
2. Who was first in her life?
3. Should we still pray, even in our sinful nature **OR** continue to sin and act as if God does not exist because of our repeated offenses?
4. What lessons have you learned from this chapter?
5. What principles could you apply to your life?

Scriptures and Prayer

For broken promises: "It is better that you should not vow than that you should vow and not pay" (Ecclesiastes 5:5, ESV).

Having premarital sex: "But if they cannot exercise self-control, they should marry. For it is better to marry than to burn with passion" (1 Corinthians 7:9, ESV).

Trust no man. Trust God: "Praise the Lord! Praise the Lord, O my soul! I will praise the Lord as long as I live; I will sing praises to God while I have my being. Put not your trust in princes, in a son of man, in whom there is no salvation" (Psalm 146:1-3, ESV).

Keep the faith: "So, faith comes from hearing, and hearing through the Word of Christ" (Romans 10:17, ESV).

Prayer:

Father, in the name of Jesus, I ask that You help to right my wrongs. Moving forward and with Your help, I will not be a repeat offender unto you, Lord. I will put and keep You first as Headship over my life. Please forgive me for my past sins. I thank you in advance.

Amen.

Never Again—But Wait… Did You Consult God?

Pen Your Prayer

Chapter Two

Making decisions without God's guidance can leave you broken, damaged, and crippled in unthought-of ways. In everything you do, keep God first.

Never Again—But Wait... Did You Consult God?

On November 21st, I gave birth to a beautiful baby girl I named Maxine. Her presence in my life brightened my days after living in a state of darkness for so many years. My best friend of five years, Issac, was with me every step of the way.

As time passed, my hatred for Kendrick grew stronger and stronger. As my hatred for him grew, I could not put my life in the right perspective. I couldn't be tied down to an infant, work, and care for my other children simultaneously, so I decided to send my daughter, Maxine, to live with my childless aunt and uncle until I could get my life to resemble some type of order. In the process, I also put Issac out of the apartment we shared because, at every turn, I thought he and everyone else was out to get and use me.

I knew deep down in my heart that Issac was in love with me and loved me as more than a best friend, but let me be real for a moment: He just wasn't my "type." My type seemed to be the man who had no sense of direction in life and only looked out for himself. I liked my men dark, a little on the heavy side, with gold teeth—and very dominant.

My life didn't seem to have the firm foundation it once had. If I were to compare my life to a house, the house would be classified as more stable than my life. It was as if every day when I woke up, I was faced with another World War — but it was only me against me.

That following January, life as I knew it changed forever. I met a man named Davin at a carwash in Gainesville, Florida, who was just released from prison. I wasn't looking for love at the time; it found me. As I prepared to gather coins from the coin machine to wash my car, I could feel someone staring at me. I turned around with somewhat of a frown on my face, only to find him standing there right behind me. I quickly turned back around and asked (to no one in particular), "What in the world is he looking at?"

Bring on the "small talk."

Davin: *"What is a beautiful young lady like yourself doing at a car wash?"*

Me: *"Duh. About to wash my car."*

Davin: *"Well, if I was your man, you wouldn't have to wash your car. I would do it for you."*

Me: *"Well, you are not my man. Have a nice day."*

Davin: *"I'm not going to stop bothering you until you look at me and talk to me."*

Me: *"I will have to talk to you when I finish doing what I came to do. Talking to you was not part of it."*

Davin(laughing): *"I will be waiting for you to finish."*

Now, in my mind, I was saying how cute he was—but he was **SO AGGRAVATING!**

Lord! Why didn't I just keep going?!

When I finished washing my car, I quickly jumped in and prepared to pull away. Well, I didn't have to go to him when I was done because he made sure I didn't get away. That day, we laughed and talked for quite a while. When I asked him why such an attractive man didn't have a lady, he responded, *"I just got out of prison for attempted murder."*

At that moment, it felt as though my heart fell out of my body and onto the hot ground on which I stood. Did my soul leave my body—running, not flying?

I swallowed hard before asking my next question (I am sure my eyes were almost bulging out of my head). I had to know more, though. *"Davin, how did you do that? Why? What took you there?"* My first instinct was to grab my keys off the hood of my car, jump in, and leave, but I didn't do that. I did not want him to pick up on just how afraid I was, so I stood there looking fearless and played it off. As time passed, the heat of the day began to feel like fire falling from the sun. We exchanged numbers and, before parting ways, he pleaded with me to call him. I told him I would call, but honey, after getting an earful of his life, I planned on tossing his number and moving on with my life.

For three weeks, I refused to answer or return his calls. He seemed to be a thirst trap…at least until the day came when I felt lonely and in need of some sinful attention, so I called him.

I now understand when the Bible says, *"The spirit is willing, but the flesh is weak."* It was then I knew I was soon to put into practice what some men do to women all the time: lay with them with no feelings attached.

Chapter 2 Points to Ponder

1. Does it appear that Kenya hates Kendrick or herself for how things turned out between them?
2. Kenya gave Maxine to her childless aunt and uncle. Why do you think she didn't allow them to keep her other four children?
3. Why is it that when we see a situation clear as day, we do not take heed and move on?

Scripture

For fulfilling the needs of the flesh: "And He came to the disciples and found them sleeping. And He said to Peter, 'So, could you not watch with me one hour? Watch and pray that you may not enter into temptation. The spirit indeed is willing, but the flesh is weak'" (Matthew 26:40-41 (ESV).

Never Again—But Wait... Did You Consult God?

Pen Your Prayer

_____
_____
_____
_____
_____
_____
_____
_____
_____
_____
_____
_____
_____
_____
_____
_____
_____
_____
_____
_____

Chapter Three

Something that feels so good physically can become deadly to your spirit. Always learn from your mistakes, and never repeat them.

Never Again—But Wait… Did You Consult God?

Some time went by, and one piece of Davin's clothing turned into two pieces. The next thing I knew, he was totally moved into my place. Being that he didn't have any children, it was he who suggested I bring Maxine back home. Davin had a love for children, and they had a love for him. Although he didn't have any children of his own, he was attached to a little girl named Reginae who was five years old when he first went to prison for the attempted murder charge. He was close to her because she was just a toddler when he went in. Now that he was out of prison, she would call his phone and he would bring her to our home (she was a teen at that point).

I made sure to shut down the "situation" as soon as I began to see the signs. Davin's family had already told him the very same things I said: If he didn't keep Reginae from around him, he would end up back in prison because of her infatuation with him. Nonetheless, their relationship was long-lived — and I now realize why it was so. (Kenya takes a break to cry…)

Davin was a good-looking man who knew how to scratch the itch that I needed in the bedroom. He was also a hustler. Not only did he know how to cut hair, but he also sold marijuana before "graduating" to cocaine.

In October of that same year, I was served notice that I had to vacate my 3-bedroom apartment on account of Davin's bad choices. He went from being a dish washer at Red Lobster to being just another dope dealer, hungry for that next dollar to feed his greed — not caring at all who he hurt in the process. As long as he was satisfied, that was all that mattered.

During our time together, crazy calls and texts began to appear on his phone. Shortly after, he started to verbally abuse me. I knew I should have let him leave the many times he tried, but "crazy me" couldn't let him get away. Nope. The last man who did that left me caring for his "package." I said to myself, *"If anyone leaves, it will be me — and that will be when I get sick and tired of him!"*

It's funny how life works. I went from being his fool to being almost homeless. We moved into his mother's double-wide trailer in the small town of Hawthorne, Florida, which was on the outskirts of Gainesville. The area was way out of my jurisdiction. Much like the typical abuser, he also kept me isolated from my family and friends. Every call I made was monitored, and every visit made was short. The coolness from him was so heavy, any time I sought just a moment of happiness or dared to smile in his presence, that feeling of joy quickly diminished.

Never Again—But Wait… Did You Consult God?

I felt myself slowly giving in completely to Davin. The prayers I thought were being answered actually felt as if they were bouncing off the wall and back to me with the message attached:

"RETURN TO SENDER."

The more I cried out for his love, the drunker it seemed he would get. The more I screamed for family time, the longer he stayed out until he knew everyone in the home was asleep. The more I said, *"I love you,"* the more he found fault in my love.

I truly did not know if I was coming or going. All I knew with surety was that I lived on his turf and had to play his way, or my children and I would truly be homeless. I hoped he would change. I believed if I did not complain about all the wrong things he did, he would notice I was a good woman to and for and him. Sadly, he never noticed because he was knee deep in his own sinful pleasures.

He was in and out of jail from the first time we met until our very last encounter. As a matter of fact, when he went to jail, I was the one who bailed him out. When he did wrong, I brushed it under the rug like it never happened.

Call me stupid if you must. I call it a lesson learned.

At the time, all I owned were two cars, furniture, and the clothes on my back. I had no place to call my very own. It didn't help to easy my discomfort by knowing Davin was loved by a lot of people, especially children. It was almost like they could relate to him and be their authentic selves. He was the "cool uncle" (as his niece and nephews would say), and he was somewhat of a legend a community that appeared to be looking for some form of a superhero. I wished I felt what they did...

That, however, wasn't my reality. When we were around others, he smiled so big, everyone could see how deep his dimples were. Whenever I said something to him, however, he gave me a look that said, *"Shut up and know your position!"*

One thing's for sure: Never say *"NEVER!"* Hold your rock, my friend! There is more to come!

Chapter 3 Points to Ponder

1. Can you recall a time when you said there was something you would NEVER do?
2. Why does it appear that we notice things when others are going through, but when it's us, it is harder to see?

Prayer

Lord, help Your people to see clearly — both physically and spiritually. Every hidden thing that surrounds them, please reveal it to them so that they can boldly walk away from toxic and deadly situations, much like I went through. Please allow them to reach out to get the help they need before it is too late.

In Jesus' Name I pray,

Amen.

Never Again—But Wait... Did You Consult God?

Pen Your Prayer

Chapter Four

Never attempt to take something that was never yours to take in the first place. Once you are gone, you are GONE. There is no forgiveness after that.

Never Again—But Wait... Did You Consult God?

December came in the blink of an eye, and I was at a standstill in my life. Davin's indiscretions became more noticeable, and I called him out on them Our relationship was taking its toll and a wrong turn. I used to blame myself for his shortcomings. I used to make excuses for the things he would do wrong to and towards me.

If you are reading this and are one who makes excuses for your abuser, **STOP**...and **RUN**!

Everything I said I would **NEVER** put up with when I was young and watching the women go through in my family are things I, too, went through. I later discovered to never say "NEVER." Instead, my words changed to, *"Lord willing, I will not have to ever go through that."*

I remember the following day as clear as the skies above. **"I know what you are up to!"** I hollered as I laid with my head propped on a pillow leaned back against the headboard.

He turned to me in a flash with fire in his eyes and asked sarcastically, *"Kenya, what am I up to — since you know so much? You don't have a clue, do you?"*

I wanted to cry but did not want to show any sign of weakness. He was slowly but surely breaking me down emotionally and physically. Emotionally, I constantly felt like "less than." My decisions were unstable, and I often cried because I noticed the relationship had given me low self-esteem. Physically, I could not sleep. His aggressiveness and beatings made me curse the day I was born. I just wanted to get it over with and die.

When I didn't respond to his newest berating, his voice grew more boisterous as he demanded an answer.

I wanted to burst out in tears like a baby, pack what I could into one of the cars, grab my children, and beg my mom for forgiveness for not keeping in constant contact with her because of him. I was ready to tell my mom everything Davin did to me and tell her she was right, but I was afraid to leave. Plus, I did not want to start over with another relationship. By that point, I knew I wasn't in love with Davin and that it was a relationship of mere convenience.

Do you know that by staying in a toxic and abusive relationship, it can cost you your very life if you are not careful and do not find a way of escape?

Eventually, I found my voice, inhaled deeply, and shouted with surety, **"Oh, don't worry about it. Just know that I know. I will soon expose you for who you truly are!"**

He smiled smugly, opened his arms wide, and said, *"Kenya, you have no idea, do you? There's nothing you can do to me. You're in my neck of the woods. You and your kids are the ones who are homeless. I have somewhere to stay!"*

Let me pause here for just a second to tell you that in my mind, I wanted to go tsunami on him! I had an out-of-body experience like no other. **How dare he mock my circumstances that way!!!** After all, I would not have been homeless had it not been for his "extra-curricular activities" that got him arrested in my car and them putting my government-subsidized apartment address on his arrest papers that led to me being evicted! **How dare he!!!**

I snapped back to reality and thought to myself, *"He's right. Where would I go? Who can I turn to? He made sure all the people who loved me would not welcome me back with open arms."* Much like a matchstick house that would quickly burn down when the first match was lit, Davin made sure my relationships were irreparably destroyed.

When he knew I was truly fed up with him and his antics, he started beating me more and more. As well, there was information he had that was being leaked by someone close to me, proving to fuel his anger. He would blurt out things that he should not know—unless someone close to me at the time told him. It **couldn't** have been any of my children because *OUR* bonds were super close, so whoever was telling Davin my "stuff" was feeding it to him all kinds of wrong.

I recall one Saturday night, he did his usual: go to the club and return in the wee hours of the morning. On that particular night, I decided to go and look for him…and my car. I was ready to show my tail because I was up waiting for him and was tired of him doing whatever he wanted to do. I woke up Lynderia to ride with me, just in case I located my car and needed her to drive it back to the house.

Well, lo and behold, I found my car parked in front of a white fenced-in mobile home. It appeared all the lights were off inside. I blew my horn, called Davin's phone (no answer), and then blew my horn again, hoping he would come out. He didn't. I then instructed Lynderia to get in the car he drove and prepare to drive off. She, however, suggested I wait to talk to

Davin because maybe — *just maybe* — he was with his running partner inside and had fallen asleep. I didn't want to hear it.

By the time she decided to get into the car Davin had driven to the trailer, and just as I prepared to get into my car, I looked up and saw not one but **FOUR** people coming out of the trailer: Davin and three women. Davin yelled at me. I yelled back at Davin full of rage and assured him that I was *DONE*. He swung the gate open, grabbed me with one of his bare hands, and began to choke and slam me on the hood of various cars, all while telling me to shut up and go home. Lynderia had grabbed a hold of his arms and begged him to stop. All the while, the other women just stood there watching, not doing anything to assist to diffuse the situation.

When Davin finally turned me loose, Lynderia got into the other car and we drove away with her following behind me. I cried all the way home. Not long after, one of his side chicks dropped him off. I hurried into the house and began to pack. When he came into the room, he closed the door behind him and started fussing and fighting with me, telling me that if I leave him, he will kill me — words I had never heard spoken from his lips before. I grew instantly terrified and filled with all the ***"What if?"*** questions you can likely imagine. (Kenya pauses writing to take another break…)

While growing up, I don't recall **ever** seeing a toxic relationship like the one I was in. The abuse was so bad, it got to the point where he would draw guns, aim, and shoot the bullets into the air. He then swore to me, *"The next one will not miss if you don't do as I say!"*

It was almost like I was in a nightmare and could not wake up.

That morning (following the trailer incident), instead of me taking the smaller children to the bus stop, Davin took on the task — and also took my keys so that I couldn't go anywhere. When he returned home, he wanted to have sex with me. We fussed and fought because I did not want to be touched by him. He had hurt me, embarrassed me, and took my love for granted. I was tired of it all and simply ready to find some sort of sunshine to brighten my dark days. He then started to scream at me as if I were a child, which led to us wrestling. He tore off my clothes in the process and forced me to have sex with him — the same manner in which a rapist does their victim. Crying was of no use because I was in "his world" and had to play my part or "get dealt with."

I wanted to die. I felt violated and so far away from God, I just knew there was no way I could turn to Him for help because I had disappointed Him for the last time. Suicide was the only way out of my misery. I consumed a handful of pills while sitting in my car and then drove away and hid where no one would ever find me until it was too late.

When I began feeling dizzy, lightheaded, and my fingers and thighs started getting a tingling sensation, I knew "a never-ending sleep" was soon to come. I cried out to God and prayed — and He answered me lovingly:

"Kenya, if you kill yourself, the world will not stop. The problem you think you are having is petty because Davin will continue doing the same thing whether you are dead or alive."

In Matthew 7:7, it says, *"Ask, and it will be given to you; seek, and you will find; knock, and it will be open to you."*

I pleaded and asked the Lord to forgive me, help me to get out of that relationship, and to shed light on anything going on around me that wasn't right.

Well, I asked and now know the Lord's Word will never return to me void.

Chapter 4 Points to Ponder

1. Why is it that some women will risk being in a toxic relationship or marriage because of not wanting to start over?
2. Do you think it is love when someone puts their hands on another forcibly?
3. What would you suggest to someone who needs a way of escape from being victimized?

Prayer

Most Gracious Father, we thank You now for Your protection. I believe that at this point in my reader's reading, the spirit of convection has overcome those who are going through similar situations. Lord, You did not create us to hurt one another but to love one another. I pray even now that every victim reading this will find a way of escape.

In Your Precious Name we pray,

Amen.

Pen Your Prayer

Chapter Five

God will never leave His children; His children leave Him. Just because you got knocked down does not mean you are knocked out.

After God saved me from me, my prayer then became, "*Save me from Davin.*" My prayer life became stronger. In January, I started having visions but could not discern what the Holy Spirit was trying to tell me. I had always been gifted in that area. One of my earliest memories of using the gift was when, at the age of four, I helped Gainesville Police Department find the weapon that was used to try and kill my uncle.

Meanwhile, my love for Davin was fading away slowly. It got to the point where I couldn't even stand being anywhere around him. A few times, when he came home drunk in the wee hours of the morning, as soon as he would get in the bed, I would get out of it, get into my car, and ride down the dark dirt road that his mother's trailer was on. I would then hide my car in the bushes and sleep the night away, just to make him mad or have him thinking I spent some time with another man.

During one of those in-car stays, I had a very vivid dream. In it, Jesus and I were floating mid-air. As I looked down, it was as if the roof on the trailer had been peeled back like a can.

Jesus said to me, "*See Davin? He is sleeping with no worries nor cares.*" He then directed my focus on the rear of his mother's

3-bedroom mobile home and said, *"See Lynderia? She is resting. Now, look at the other children. They are crying out for you. They miss you. They need you."*

The other children were pounding on the window, looking out and crying for me to come home. Even after that, I was still unable to put two and two together. When my spirit returned to my car, I woke up and went straight home. Everything was just as Jesus had shown me in the vision.

You name it, I have been through it. It has been only by the grace of God that death couldn't touch me before my time. When death is afraid of laying hands on you, there must be a greater calling on your life.

Before I moved, I knew something had to give. I began to find condoms hidden under the speakers the car he was driving (and sometimes loaned out to his friend). I got him hired where I was working, and he got fired for having so many sexual complaints. Hear him tell it, everybody was lying on him and were jealous of how good he looked. I knew the young ladies were telling the truth, and, in a sense, I was seeking a valid reason to be released from him. Then, it got worse because that same company found a reason to fire me as well!

I questioned Davin often, asking, *"If I am giving you everything, why do you do such things? Why do you keep hurting the children and me?"* I never received a straight answer. He simply brushed it off, just like he did everything else.

His mother tried to get me to leave him several times. There were times she would come and get me to ride with her to different places. While riding, she would ask me a series of questions, with the bottom line being that her son was not the man for me and that my children and I would be better off without him. She even stated Davin carried a curse over his life. Every time, my response to her was that I loved him and that he needed a woman like me who understood him. It was almost like his mother was saying something without really **SAYING** it.

I also knew his mother was not too fond of me. She knew I was too good for her son, but being that I was a young, unwed mother, she likely thought I was beneath her. I recall the night she stopped by the house and knocked on the door with urgency. ***"I need to speak to my son, Kenya."***

For whatever reason, Davin had been dodging his mother. When I told him she was there, he didn't want to get up. He hated when his mother would just "pop up." However, I begged for him to see what his mother wanted, which he did.

As I approached from behind, I could hear his mother crying. She repeatedly asked him, *"What is happening to you?"* She was there trying to save her son's life. When she told him that whatever he was doing, he needed to stop, it was as if a dark, evil mist seemed to fall on his face that not even he could shake off. She kept crying and beating on his chest, begging him to stop walking hand-in-hand with the devil. Before she left, she told him with surety, *"The devil has a hold on you, and you are headed back to prison."*

At the time, I thought she was just putting her mouth on him wrong, but how many know that a mother truly knows her seed? That moment was not to be forgotten, for the truth would soon unravel.

Chapter 5 Points to Ponder

1. Is there an area of your life where God has shown you warning signs and you ignored them?
2. In what ways can you begin to implement change in your life for the better of you and your family?

Prayer

Dear God, please help us to embrace moving on, even if that means we must feel alone while doing so.

In Jesus' Name we pray,

Amen.

Author Kenya Herring-Walker

Pen Your Prayer

Chapter Six

Sometimes, it takes something so breathtaking to make you do right.

I was used and abused in more ways than one by Davin. Being mindful that he wasn't holding a steady, legal job while we were together, there were times when he used to host big cookouts—at the expense of my children and me. Other times, the women he cheated on me with came to the house, and Davin would laugh and think it was cool to make such a foul move. I refused to let his women win by turning him loose because of them, so I continued to live in misery…and danger.

At the time, we had moved out of his mother's home and into our own place. I used to keep track of his phone records, just to find an excuse to turn off his phone—that I was paying for. One time, after doing so, he came home enraged. He made the mistake of putting his hands on me while I was in the kitchen. He began choking me and, at one point, had me dangling mid-air. I swung my body back and forth, trying to reach something to hit him with. I finally got a hold of a pan with sharp edges and bashed him across the eye. All I saw was blood as he released me.

He backed away and yelled, *"Kenya, now you have drawn blood! I am going to kill you!"*

Never Again—But Wait... Did You Consult God?

I don't know where my sudden burst of energy came from, but **THAT** night, I was about to give Davin what his mama should have given him years ago: a whooping he would never forget, even if it meant him being taking out in a body bag. I was sick and tired of his abuse! I screamed for my children to call 911. By the time the police arrived, Davin had fled. He came back the next day, and we went about our lives as if the night before didn't even happen...but it did.

Later that night, our argument turned into another fight. By that time, I was physically, emotionally, and spiritually tired of going back and forth with him. He cornered me in a room with a sawed-off shotgun and aimed it at my head as three of my five children cried and pleaded for him to stop. I heard glass shattering amid everyone screaming at the top of their lungs. When he swung the gun in an attempt to hit me with the wooden party of the handle, my children covered my body like pillows, preventing him from getting to me. My one-year-old daughter grabbed his leg and screamed, *"Daddy! Daddy!"* so that he would stop. It seemed the more difficulty he had getting to me, the more power I gave him. When I realized my children could get hurt during the altercation, I made them get off me and run as far as they could to get help.

Once I knew they were safe, I got on my knees, closed my eyes, and began to pray, asking God to remove Davin from my life once and for all. As I prayed, the prison flashed before my eyes. I begged the Lord not to send Davin back there, but He told me, *"Now, you have put this situation in My hands."*

While still on my knees, I told Davin that I didn't care what he did to me — and I meant it. I also said to him, *"Either way, you still lose."* He might have hurt me or killed my body, but God would have my soul. By the time I stopped praying and opened my eyes, he was gone.

I was very shaken by that incident. It was the one time I stood my ground and called the police to have him arrested. His friend, Bryce, came by to get the gun and remove it from the house, all while telling me I should not have called the police. Yes, he basically condoned Davin's bad behavior. (True friends do not cover you when you're wrong. They call you out on it so that you can become better.) It was then I chose to finally tell a family member what Davin had done to me. I refrained from doing so earlier because I learned to not get people involved in my relationships, especially when there's even a remote chance that I would get back with "him." Meanwhile, my family and friends would still be holding onto a grudge behind what was done to me. It was best to keep silent until…

I called my sister, Anita, who arrived at my house by the time Davin was placed in the police car. She wanted to fight him so bad. Anita even said, *"I knew you were done with him when you called me."* In my mind, I was sure. I could **FINALLY** get a decent night of rest.

When Davin went to court, I did not go to his first appearance. I knew he would try to call me, professing how much he needed my help — which he did. Yet again, I helped him by posting bail. The difference was **THAT** time, he did not return to my house. After all, I had a case against him.

You can *NEVER* underestimate the power of God and what He can do.

Chapter 6 Points to Ponder

1. Why do we (as people) turn back to our vomit (situations that are not good for us)?
2. When do you know when you have truly had enough?

Prayer

Father, we thank You for Your hedge of protection. Lord, we thank You for loving us beyond our sinful nature. We thank You for giving us a way of escape. You told us that no weapon formed against us shall prosper and that Your Word will never return to us void. Thank You, Abba.

In Jesus Name we pray,

Amen.

Author Kenya Herring-Walker

Pen Your Prayer

Chapter Seven

Love does not hurt. Love does not have a respect of person. It just embraces whoever it can. However, know there is a thin line between love and hate.

Your mouth might have dropped to the floor when you learned I bailed Davin out of jail. I know. I know. Crazy, right? We did, however, agree to separate for a little while until everything cooled off. Before long, I found myself missing him. I cried. I prayed. Then, I called him. I wanted him lying next to me and to fix what was broken between us.

Later that night, I saw him at the store. The very instant I saw him, I felt something odd in my spirit but couldn't put my finger on it. He didn't know I saw him, though. When I got home, I called him, and he came over to the house. Once there, he asked me to return to the store for him because he forgot to grab himself a beer while he was out. My spirit told me, *"No, he didn't,"* but I convinced myself to do what he asked to keep the peace. I rushed out the door, went to the store, and grabbed him a beer. All the while, something deep on the inside of me did not feel right.

On my way back home, the Holy Spirit spoke and told me to ease into the yard with the lights off and park close to the end of the driveway. I used to be terrified of the dark, so I ignored the voice and drove all the way up the driveway as usual. I turned the music down and could hear someone running through my mobile home. I hurried to exit the car and ran into the house to see what all the noise was about. All the children were asleep, and Davin was in the shower.

Who, then, was running through my house?!

I pulled back the shower curtain and told him I was home. He stood in the shower, looking at me as if he wanted to tell me something but didn't quite know how to say it. I smiled and said to him, seductively, *"What's wrong? Do you want me to join you?"*

The expression on his face never changed when he told me yes. So, I joined him, and, as the water rolled off his face, he looked deep into my eyes and asked me, *"Why do you love me?"* I replied with my honest answer of, *"Because I love you,"* to which he replied, *"I love you, too."*

Once we got out of the shower, he took only a sip of the beer he said he *needed*. We then had intercourse before he called his friend to pick him up. While we waited, he sat on the edge of my bed and started crying. *"Davin, what's wrong?"* I asked with genuine concern.

Before he could respond, the Holy Spirit said, *"Kenya, he has something to tell you, but what he is about to say is going to be a lie."*

When Davin spoke, he said, *"Kenya, I think I have cancer."*

The Holy Spirit within me kept chanting, ***"LIES! LIES! LIES!"***

His crying was out of control, to the point that Lynderia stirred out of her sleep and heard him. She came into the room to embrace him, but I sent her back to bed. Not long after, his ride came to pick him up. We hugged and kissed goodbye before parting ways.

Something still did not feel right, though. I could not shake the uneasy feeling in my spirit.

Chapter 7 Points to Ponder

1. Whether you call it "gut instinct" or "spirit speak," what do you do when you feel it and it goes against what you believe?
2. Do you always listen to that instinct? If not, what deters you?
3. What are some of the consequences of not listening to that voice?

Prayer

Father God, thank You for the presence of Your Holy Spirit in our lives. Thank You for not turning Your back on us, even when we come to you occasionally. Please forgive us for our selfish belief that we can do everything all on our own, knowing that only with You, all things are possible.

In Jesus' Mighty Name we pray,

Amen.

Pen Your Prayer

Chapter Eight

Always remember: When God does something, it is for your good.

Never Again—But Wait… Did You Consult God?

The next day, around 5:00 a.m., I went to where Davin was staying temporarily—his sister's house. We laid down for a few hours and, of course, had intercourse again before I drove Davin to his appointment with his probation officer and then to a class at the State Attorney's Office that would help to have the assault charges dropped. It seemed to me that everything was working out just as Davin planned.

Until...

While I was waiting for him to come out of the probation office, the wait seemed just a little too long. I was soon to learn why.

The probation officer approached my car and told me Davin was not returning the same way he came. He went on to suggest that I do a thorough background check on Davin because I obviously didn't know who he truly was. I didn't know whether to cry or play "Bonnie" and bail him out that very instant. I ended up leaving there, feeling defeated yet again.

Later, Davin called home and told me he hoped he would get a bond when he made his first appearance. I responded that no matter what, I loved him and would wait for him.

As my tears tried to drown my sorrow, it began to feel as if I was on the verge of a nervous breakdown. He was all I knew and breathed. I all but forgot how he had pulled a gun on me, cheated on me, physically abused me, and practically raped me. I planned on riding out his bid with him.

Never Again—But Wait… Did You Consult God?

DAVIN'S IN-PRISON MARRIAGE PROPOSAL
(Page 1)

BEGINNING PROCEDURES FOR MARRIAGE

The inmate's fiancée must write a letter stating that (1) she wishes to marry the inmate and (2) why. The letter must also include her (3) date of birth, (4) age, (5) Social Security Number, (6) marital status, and (7) address. Please make sure the letter is (8) signed and dated. If the fiancée is divorced, she must (9) provide a copy of her divorce document.

LETTER REQUESTING TO MARRY WHILE INCARCERATED

✓ If either the inmate or his fiancée have been previously married, documentation of Dissolution of Marriage is required. Likewise, if either the Inmate or fiancée's previous spouse is deceased documentation of Death Certificate is required.

✓ The Inmate must provide a letter containing the same information as stated above.

✓ If the name of the Inmate's fiancée is not on his approved visiting list, the Marriage Request will be delayed until her name is placed on the Inmate's visiting list.

✓ Subsequent to receiving the aforementioned letter from both the Inmate and his fiancée, security must complete an evaluation and the Inmate will be placed on call-out for completion of a Psychology Consultation.

✓ NOTE: The Inmate must attach the requested information (letter) to an Inmate Request Form and forward it to Chaplain Hendricks.

✓ NOTE: The fiancée must mail the requested information to the address listed below:

    Attention: Chaplain David Hendricks
                       Graceville Correctional Facility
                       5168 Ezell Road
                       Graceville, Florida 32440

Author Kenya Herring-Walker

DAVIN'S IN-PRISON MARRIAGE PROPOSAL
(Page 2)

STATE OF FLORIDA
DEPARTMENT OF CORRECTIONS
GRACEVILLE CORRECTIONAL INSTITUTION

REQUEST TO MARRY

On this date, I request approval to marry my fiancé/fiancée while I am still in the custody of the Florida Department of Corrections.

INMATE NAME: ███████████████ DC# A-███████

HAS THE INMATE EVER BEEN PREVIOUSLY MARRIED? ___ Yes ✓ No

FIANCÉ/FIANCÉE NAME: Ms. Kenya ███████████

IS THE FIANCÉ/FIANCÉE CURRENTLY UNDER AGE OF 18? ___ Yes ✓ No

HAS THE FIANCÉ/FIANCÉE EVER BEEN PREVIOUSLY MARRIED? ___ Yes ✓ No

If approved to marry, I understand that my fiancé/fiancée and I will be responsible for the following:

1. Making the application for the marriage license and arrangements for necessary forms to be sent to the inmate for application;
2. Making arrangements for the ceremony in coordination with the Chaplain;
3. All costs involved

I confirm by my signature that the information provided above is true and accurate to the best of my knowledge.

Inmate Signature: ███████████████ Date: May 22, 2009

Fiancé/Fiancée Signature: _____ Date: _____

Received by Chaplain _____ on _____

8 (11/06)

Never Again—But Wait… Did You Consult God?

I didn't know how I would break the news to the children that Davin would be out of their lives for a while, especially Lynderia. She and Davin had a close relationship, so it was Lynderia I told first. She responded by collapsing on the porch, kicking her feet back and forth like a baby whose bottle had been taken from them. I cried with her as I embraced her, trying to reassure her that everything would be alright.

When her siblings came home, I shared the news with them as well. They literally walked away without uttering a single word, leaving me standing there alone.

Oddly enough, Mya, Shayla, and Tylor later expressed how happy they were to finally have me all to themselves. What they said made no sense to me because they always had me to themselves. After all, Davin was never home most of the time.

As the weeks passed, I don't know who wrote Davin more: Lynderia or me. I knew she had grown close to him because many times, she expressed her joy for having him as the father she never had. It made my heart smile to know she had a male role model in her life when her Uncle William couldn't be there for her.

Whenever Davin called home, he only asked to speak to Lynderia and Maxine, not the other three. There were times I thought Lynderia was much like his spy because she would either walk off with the phone or lay under her cover and whisper the entirety of their conversation. Even after fussing at her about it at times, I still couldn't put two and two together.

The camel's back was finally broken the night Lynderia decided to sleep in one of Davin's shirts. That night, I had to put her in her place and let her know that wearing his shirt to bed was taking things a little too far. I understood she missed him, but that was not going to fly with me. As she looked at me with obvious confusion, I suddenly felt the connection with my baby girl was somehow severed.

Chapter 8 Points to Ponder

1. Are you one who can discern when others are crying out for help without outright stating their need?
2. What kind of clues can you listen for when others are not comfortable with expressing they are in danger or pain?

Scriptures

"...for God gave us a spirit not of fear but of power and love and self-control" (2 Timothy 1:7, ESV).

"Have I not commanded you? Be strong and courageous. Do not be frightened, and do not be dismayed, for the Lord your God is with you wherever you go" (Joshua 1:9, ESV).

Never Again—But Wait... Did You Consult God?

Pen Your Prayer

Chapter Nine

Even during your weakest moments, know that it was then when God carried you.

Never Again—But Wait… Did You Consult God?

The day Davin was sentenced for violating probation, I sat in that cold courtroom, shivering and embracing myself in the seat I would soon rise from after his sentencing. When they called his name, I braced myself and prayed they would be as lenient as possible. The judge gave him 13 months. I walked out of the courtroom in tears. Yet again, it felt as if my life had no sense of direction.

The following week, I went to the jail to gather his belongings before he got sent away to prison. I couldn't wait to get in the car, go through his bag, and smell his scent on his shirt. I remained in the parking lot for a while, sniffing his shirt as the tears fell. I eventually pulled myself together, set the shirt to the side, and flipped through the letters Lynderia and I had written him. I happened upon a letter written by Lynderia, and the Holy Spirit prompted me to read it. Within, she told him how much she missed him, but as I read on, I noticed she was writing to him using a code that was simple to decipher as I read through each letter…

Author Kenya Herring-Walker

LETTER FROM LYNDERIA TO DAVIN
(Page 1)

March/5/09

Dear Daddy,

I ♥ u I ♥ u

so In Love with u!

I ♥ u 4

Whats up nu chillin thinking bout you and this oc thing. I'm in oc/well in school suspention because two weeks ago on a thursday I was supposed to go to after school detention but I didn't cause I didn't have a Ride and I wasn't at school. But any-how I have wrote you two times since Friday. She probably haven't sent them off but I did. Well my mom is a Buissness women now. Now/well Let me tell you. do you Remember when she said that she is suspecting a packet well she finally got it. Wait/ I might Be getting off to Topic or what I was Telling you but I just would like to

Never Again—But Wait… Did You Consult God?

LETTER FROM LYNDERIA TO DAVIN
(Page 2)

my mom say that I can't get it till I'm sixth-teen and thats 4 years from now. may-be me and you could get it together. you get it on you arm and I get it on my leg. that would be really nice don't you think. and may-be when you get out we could get us a shirt some shoes and some shorts all white though with ▓▓▓ and me you and ▓▓▓ take pictures together. and you could find 200 dollars and get us a digital camara. well pa I gotta go but always remember that I love you.

Sincerly,

♡

4 eva

Some secrets are meant to be kept between you and God, but understand me when I tell you this: **THAT** day, everything God was trying to show me, I understood clearly—although I didn't want to accept it for what it was. Nonetheless, I embraced it instantly, especially being that blood is before mud.

As I sat in the car, I screamed at the top of my lungs and punched the roof of the car, filled with pure frustration. I then called my Mama and asked her to meet me at my house because I just discovered something that would change our lives forever.

Almost immediately after I disconnected the call from my mother, Lynderia called to let me know she was home. I asked her how her day was, and she laughed as she told me about something funny that happened. I listened but didn't really *HEAR* her. My thoughts had drifted far away from the conversation.

How do I ask her about what I knew without making her think it's her fault?

Why didn't she trust me enough to tell me?

My thoughts were interrupted by her repeatedly calling my name. I apologized and assured her I heard everything she said. Before ending the call, I asked her if there was anything she needed to tell me. She told me no.

Chapter 9 Points to Ponder

1. Do you stand with the saying, "What goes on in this house stays in this house?"
2. What potential repercussions are there for the inability to share toxic "secrets"?
3. What situation have you encountered in the past that has caused you to carry a secret to the grave?

Scripture

"For nothing is hidden that will not be made manifest, nor is anything secret that will not be known and come to light" (Luke 8:17, ESV).

Author Kenya Herring-Walker

Pen Your Prayer

Chapter Ten

When you put your total trust in the hands of men, there is a chance they will fail you.

My heart pounded heavily. Each breath I took seemed to be harder to take. The time had come to let Lynderia know that I knew…

I gathered my strength and said to her, *"No matter what happens in this life or the next, I will always have your back and listen to you first, no matter what anyone else has to say."* I then told her Davin had already told me about everything that happened between the two of them and that I didn't care about his version of the story but wanted to hear hers.

"Tell me what he said first," she responded.

"We are not playing he-said-she-said games. I want to hear your account of things that happened!" I demanded.

****

Brace yourself, my friend… What she said next would have made anyone else—woman or man—lose their ever-loving mind!

Let's Wrap This One Up!

Throughout this entire ordeal and what's to come in the continuation of my story, it was **ONLY** the grace of God that has kept me sane. Sadly, at the time of this book's release, the mother-daughter relationship between Lynderia and I is severely broken—not irreparable, but definitely damaged. I must acknowledge that most of it comes from her denial of the events that occurred as she faces the pain of the wrongs that were done to her.

Disappointingly, my story—and Lynderia's—are not uncommon. There are a host of little girls who have been subjected to "improper touches" by someone the family trusts. Now is the time to tell the enemy, ***"I WILL NEVER LET YOU BRING SEPARATION INTO MY HOUSEHOLD AGAIN, IN THE NAME OF JESUS!"***

Stay tuned for the continuation of *"NEVER AGAIN"* in 2021! Be sure to have your seatbelt at the ready!

Closing Prayer

Father, please help a family to face their fears and the truth of what's really taking place within their family unit. I pray that every pedophile be exposed and that You deal with them expeditiously. Please give that mother and father the strength to endure and speak up for their child(ren). Lord, I pray that each child be bold and speak up about how they are being violated.

Lord, I thank You for allowing me to be of help and service unto Your people.

In Jesus' Name I pray,

Amen.

About the Author

Pastor Kenya Herring-Walker is a native of Gainesville, Florida. One of her deepest desires since her youth was to reach back into her community, as well as others. She loves to worship and praise the Lord until His total presence fills the room in which she stands. She is an Ordained Pastor. Her previous place of worship was "The House of God Church," located in the beautiful city of Ocala, Florida.

Kenya has a passion for singing and writing songs. She also loves to encourage, empower, and pray for others more than herself. Seeing others **WIN** in life brings her joy, even if it means others will pass her by on their way to success. Surrounding herself with positive, Kingdom-minded individuals helps to keep her grounded and faith-focused. When asked how she is doing, she always responds gracefully with, "ALL IS WELL!" Often, she prays with others, allowing God to be the headship over all conversations. Kenya is a prayer warrior and spiritual demon-slayer who believes prayer changes people and things.

Pastor Walker is married to her best friend, who was hand-picked by the Lord: Pastor Issac D. Walker. She refers to him as her "Best Half." She has been blessed with five beautiful children—four girls and one boy. She also has five beautiful grandchildren whom she loves dearly.

www.ingramcontent.com/pod-product-compliance
Lightning Source LLC
Chambersburg PA
CBHW052113110526
44592CB00013B/1586